Hello!

My name is **Friel**.
I am a **book angel**.

Watch for me on some of the pages in your book! I will give you hints to help you grow in your life with Jesus!

See you!
Enjoy!

First Holy Communion

My life with Jesus

PAULINE
BOOKS & MEDIA

Jesus invites me...

Come to me.

I am
the Bread of Life.

I am loved by God

and I love God

... and I love
and pray for my family.

I belong to another family also:
the world-wide family of the Catholic Church.

My parish is a small part of this very big family.

The name of my parish is:

....

There are seven very precious gifts
that we can receive as members of the Church
for our life with Jesus.

These are called
the seven sacraments.

The sacraments are where we meet God
in a very real and wonderful way.
And they help us through our whole life.

 Baptism

These are the names of the seven sacraments!

 Reconciliation

Eucharist

These four are the first sacraments you receive.

 Confirmation

Marriage

These two sacraments are for those who will follow Jesus in married life or as our priests.

 Holy Orders

 Anointing of the Sick

This one is to help you if you get seriously ill.

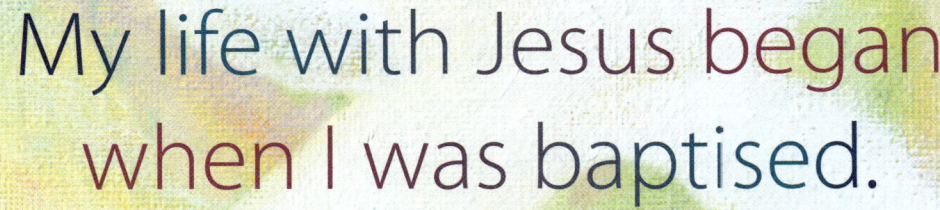

My life with Jesus began when I was baptised.

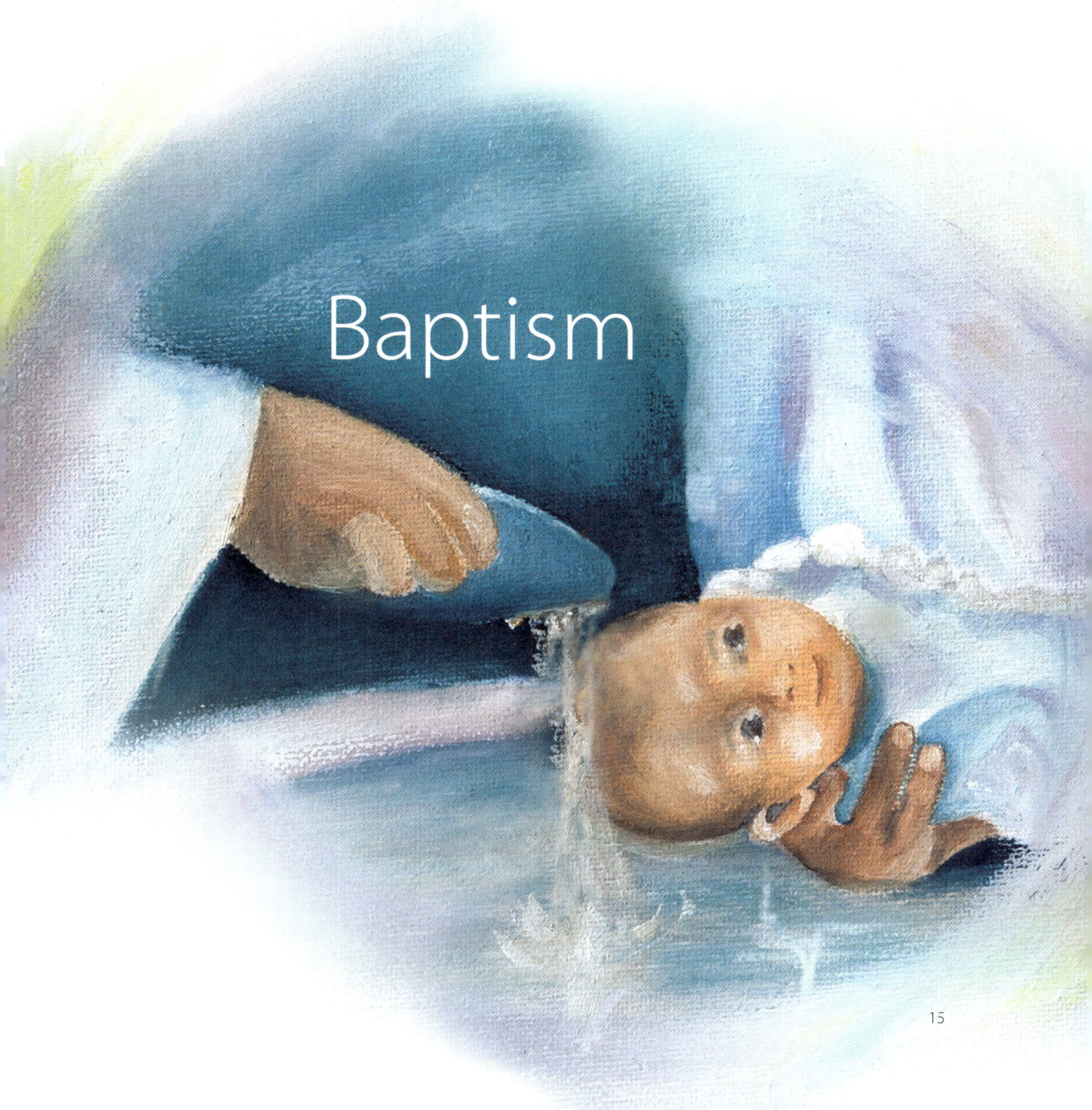

The people in my parish

My baptism made me a child of God my Father, and a member of God's world-wide family.

The name of the Church where I was baptised is

....

My baptismal name is

....

My godparents are

....

....

You were baptised
in the name of the Father
and of the Son and of the Holy Spirit.
So, when you make the Sign of the Cross,
remember that you belong to God's family.

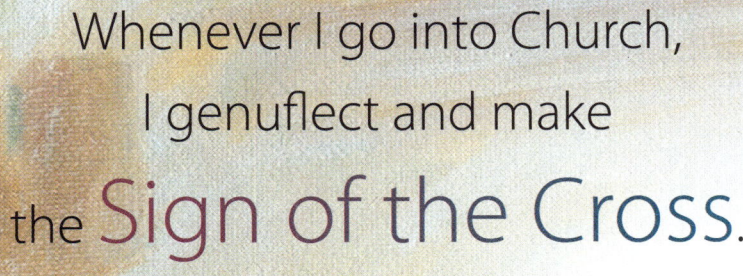

Whenever I go into Church,
I genuflect and make

the Sign of the Cross.

This reminds me that
Jesus died on the cross for me
so that I can live my life to the full!

Here is a great idea!
You can make the Sign of the Cross
as soon as you get up in the morning
and when you go to bed at night!

Jesus forgives me!

Reconciliation

My life with Jesus continued to grow
when I received
the sacrament of reconciliation
for the first time
as I prepared to receive
my first holy communion.

Jesus breathed on the apostles and said to them:

"Receive the Holy Spirit.
If you forgive the sins
of anyone
they are forgiven."

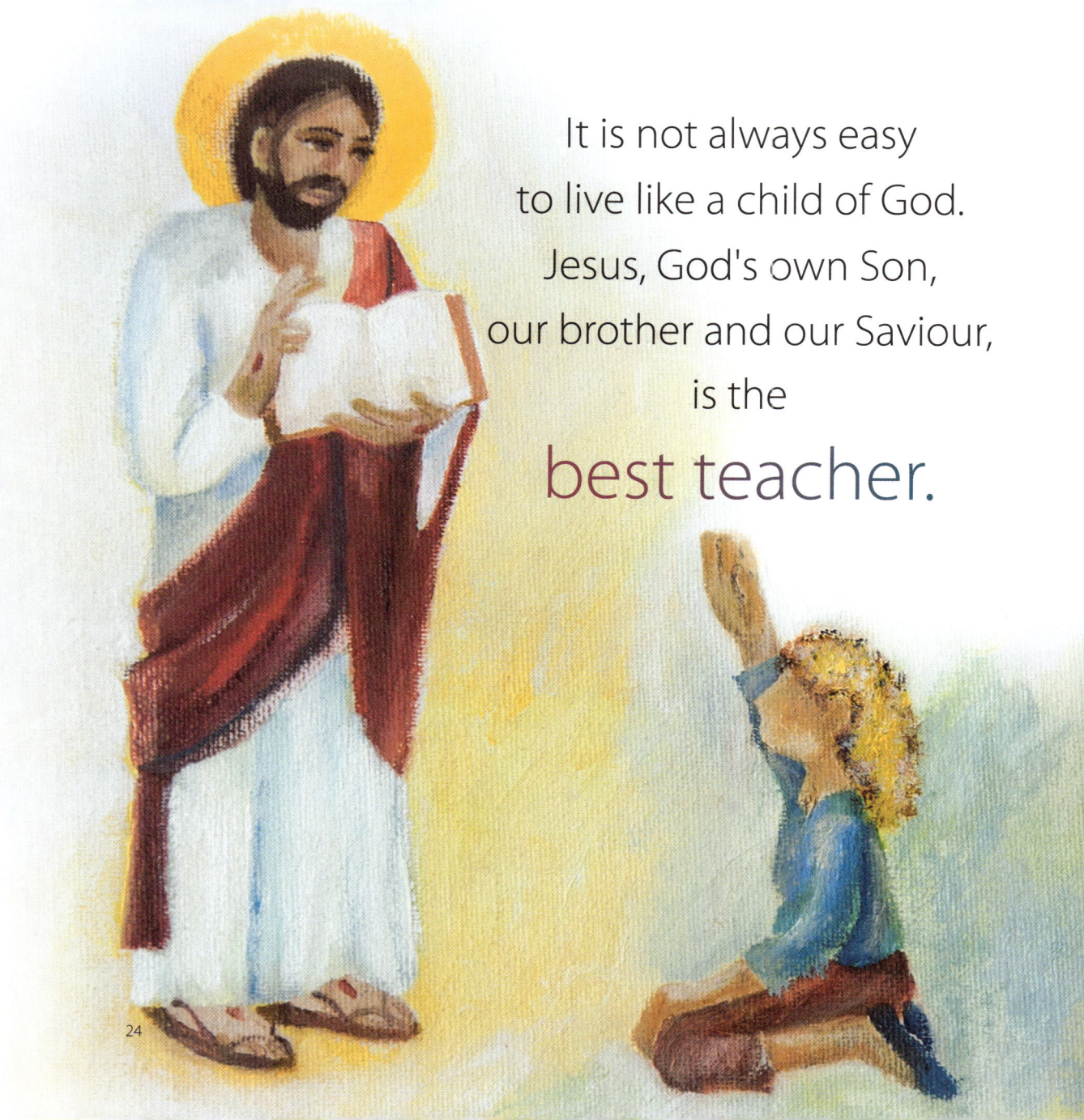

It is not always easy
to live like a child of God.
Jesus, God's own Son,
our brother and our Saviour,
is the

best teacher.

He taught us
how to live as God's children!

He not only taught us,
he showed us how!
He not only showed us how,
he helps us!

As a child of God,
I love to be the best I can be!

I want to please my parents, teachers,
and my Heavenly Father – all the time.

But, when I feel cross, sad, or just out of sorts,
I might do or say something
that hurts another person.

The sacrament of reconciliation,
where I receive
God's forgiveness
and healing,
is a real celebration!
… because God's love for me
never, ever changes!

God forgives me because God loves me – *always!*

I received the Sacrament of Reconciliation for the first time:

Date
....

Place
....

Priest
....

This is a prayer I like to say to Jesus
to thank him for his love and mercy.

Holy Communion

Jesus said:

Let the little children come to me.

Jesus is with me every day.

I received Holy Communion for the first time:

Date
....

Church
....

The name of my priest
....

At Mass we remember that Jesus celebrated the Last Supper with his disciples.

Jesus took the bread,
broke it and gave it to them saying:
This is my body.

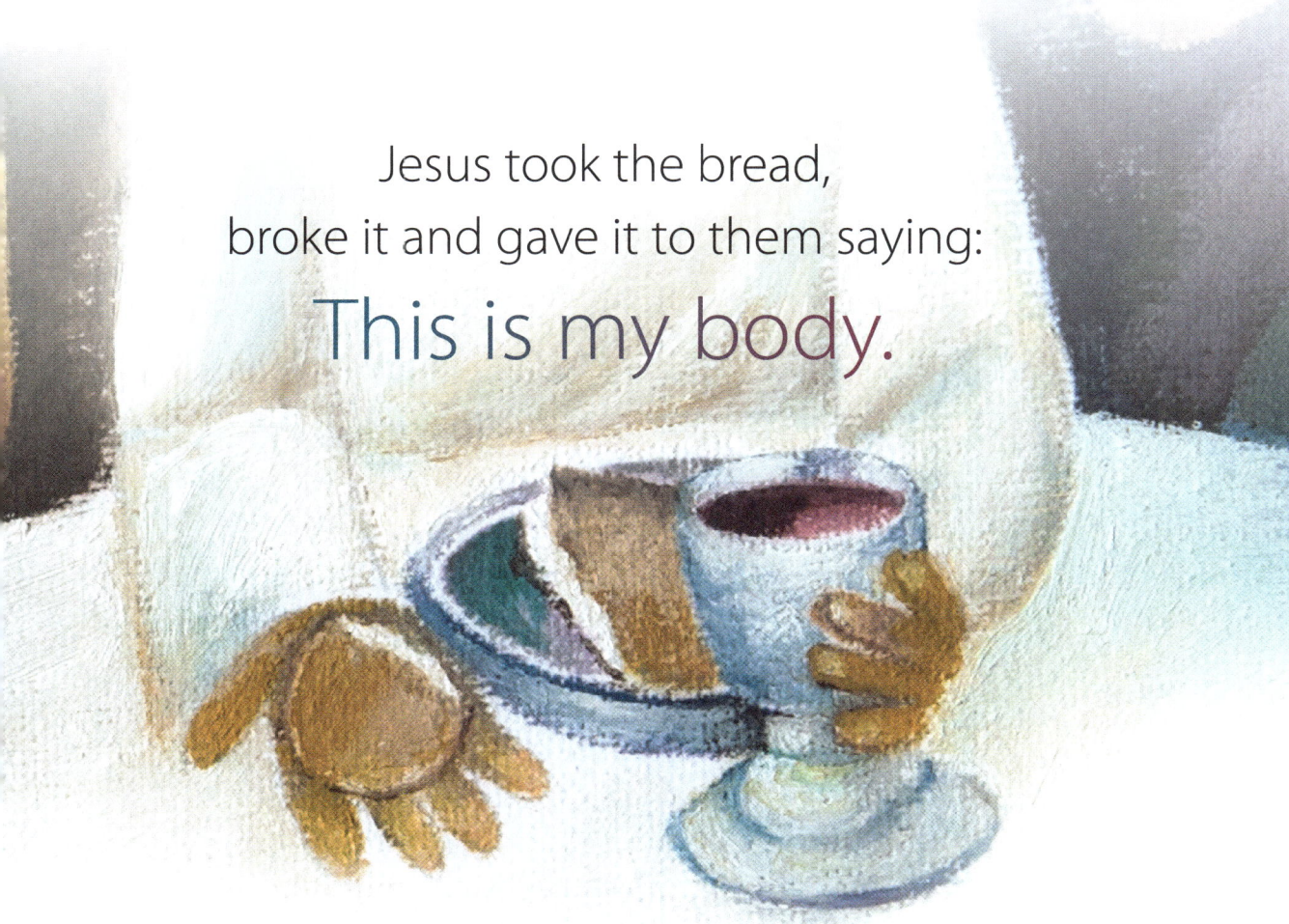

He took the chalice and gave it to his disciples:
This is the chalice
of my blood.

Through our priest and the working of the
Holy Spirit, Jesus does the same thing at every Mass.

He gives us himself in a very special way.
He does this so that we can truly share his life
and really become like him.

Every time I receive Holy Communion,
Jesus welcomes me.
He listens to my prayers.
He speaks to my heart.
He stays close to me because he really loves me!
He gives me the strength to become
the best I can be –
to be more like him!

I love Jesus!

When I receive Holy Communion

I speak to Jesus:

Praying together with others you can be sure Jesus is with you, as he promised he would be.

Jesus,

thank you for coming to me!

I tell Jesus

I love him

and

I thank him for his love.

I ask him to look after my family

and all the people I love

and all the people

in the whole world

who need his love.

Jesus is with me.

He is close to me.

Jesus listens to my prayer.

Jesus cares about my life.

And he will always answer my prayer!

Sometimes he answers me
in a way that is different from what I ask.

Because he loves us all so much
he will always answer our prayer in a way
that is best for us and the people we love.

A prayer I like to say after Holy Communion

You can write your own prayer to Jesus here!

You can use lots of colours!

My Photo Album

Psst!
This is for photos of you and your family and friends!

My First Holy Communion

Jesus is really present in the Blessed Sacrament.

I can pray to him.

I can ask his help,
for myself and for all the people I love.

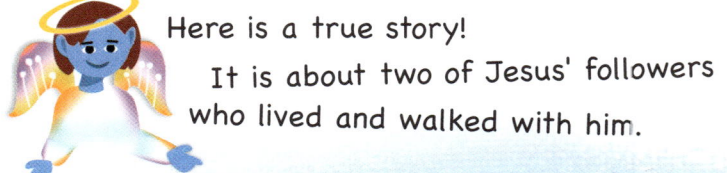

Here is a true story!
It is about two of Jesus' followers who lived and walked with him.
It is very much like your own story!

The Emmaus Journey
a true story

Emmaus is a little town near Jerusalem.
Here is how you say Emmaus:
em ay os

Two friends of Jesus were walking from Jerusalem
to a small town called Emmaus…

These two friends knew and loved Jesus.

They followed him when he went from town to town.

They listened to him when he spoke.

They thought about what he said.

They saw the way he treated people
with love and kindness
and made many sick people well again.

They were with him when he fed a crowd of thousands of people. A small child had given his disciples a few loaves of bread and some fish. Jesus took them and blessed them and fed all the people who were there.

These two disciples now were heartbroken because Jesus had been arrested and had died on the cross – a criminal's death!

They really loved Jesus and they never thought this could happen to such a good and great young man. They thought Jesus might be the One promised by God and sent to save the whole world.

They were so sad and upset that they just could not stay in Jerusalem.

They had to leave and decided early that morning to go to a small town, just about a day's walk.

When they left, they could still see the empty cross where Jesus died and it made them very, very sad.

But also, something else happened just before they left Jerusalem, and they could not understand it. They talked about this as they walked along…

When Jesus died on Friday, his friends took his body down from the cross and carried it to a tomb.
But it was too late in the day for them to prepare properly for Jesus' burial, as the next day was a holy day and they were not allowed to do any work.

But, on Sunday, very early in the morning, when some of the women came back to the tomb, they were shocked! It was open, with two angels inside, and the body of Jesus was not there!

These angels told the women he was alive!

As the two friends walked along they were talking about these things and trying to figure out what could have happened. Just then, Jesus himself came along that same road, but they did not recognise him– not even when he caught up with them.

He said hello to them.
And when he saw how very sad they were
he asked them
what was the matter
with them.

When you are upset and try to figure things out, Jesus comes and walks with you to help you understand.

They stopped walking and looked straight at him.
But, they still did not recognise him!

One of them answered him and said,
"Are you the only visitor to Jerusalem
who does not know what has happened
these last few days?"

Jesus said, "What things?"

And, sometimes,
it can also be hard
for you to recognise him!

So they told Jesus about Jesus!
They described the great things he had done,
and how the leaders of the temple and the people
had him sentenced to death and crucified him.

They also told him how sad and disappointed they
were because they had very high hopes
that Jesus was the One that God promised to send
to save the people...

On top of this, they told him that some of the women
they knew went to his tomb and found it empty,
and how some angels were there and told them that
Jesus is alive!

Jesus listened to what they said and when they finished, almost surprised, he said,
"You are so slow to understand and believe what the Bible says about the One God promised to send to save the world!"

Then Jesus began to explain to them about God's plan from the beginning of the Bible. He helped them to really understand that the Bible was about him.

Before they knew it they had arrived at the little town where they were going to stop for the night.
It looked like Jesus was going to continue on his way, so they said, "Please stay with us. It is close to evening. The day is almost over."

So Jesus went into the house with them.

When you invite him, Jesus will stay with you too!

While he was at table with them, he took the bread and blessed it and broke it and gave it to them.

Just then, they opened their eyes wide and they could see that
**this stranger was Jesus himself!
truly alive!!!**

At that moment he disappeared from their sight!

Then they said to each other right away,
"Didn't our hearts burn with deep joy while he was talking to us on the way, telling us about what God said in the Bible?"

Whenever you are at Mass, Jesus comes to you too
and he opens your eyes and your heart.
Believe and know he is alive!
Your heart too will burn with love
and you will grow in your friendship with him.

The two friends did not waste a minute!
They went straight back to Jerusalem to tell the apostles and the others what they discovered.

When they arrived, the most amazing thing happened! While they were still talking about how they met him, Jesus himself stood right there in the room with them and said "Peace"!

But they were shocked. Was this really Jesus or a dream, or even a ghost?

Jesus knew how they were feeling and told them, "Don't worry. It really is me! Have a look at my hands and my feet so you can be sure it is me – in flesh and blood. You know ghosts have no flesh and bones as you see I have."

They were so full of joy, but it was still hard to understand! This was something completely different from anything they had ever experienced before – even in their dreams!

So, Jesus asked them: "Can I have something to eat?" They gave him some cooked fish and he ate it in front of them – just to show them it was really him and not a dream or a ghost!

Then he said to them: "These are my words. I told you about myself while I was with you. Everything written about me in the Bible had to happen as God said it would..." And he opened their minds so that they were able to understand much better than they ever had understood it before.

When you are with Jesus,
he opens your mind also,
to help you
really understand
his love for all people.

Jesus then told them that they must go and tell others the Good News about him.

They could do this because they saw him!
They knew for sure that he was not dead!
He is really, fully alive!

This is Good News for everyone because
it proves that Jesus' teachings are really true!
God our loving Father has spoken to us through Jesus!

You can share your love of Jesus with others
by your goodness, your kindness and your generous love.
When you do this, the love of Jesus grows inside of you too,
and you become more like him – every day of your life.

Here are some ways that I can keep learning about Jesus and share his love with others.

Hint!! Reading about Jesus

Hint!! Talking to him!

Hint!! Paying attention at Sunday Mass

1.
2.
3.
4.
5.
6.
7.

Hint!! Saying my morning and evening prayers

Hint!! Helping others without being asked

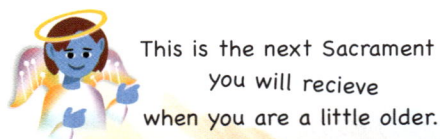 This is the next Sacrament you will recieve when you are a little older.

Confirmation

This sacrament is very important.
It completes my journey
towards full membership in the Church.

With the sacrament of Confirmation
I will receive precious gifts from the

Holy Spirit

to be able to follow Jesus as I grow up.

Confirmation will make me wise, not just smart:
to be able to see and choose
what is right,
and it will give me courage to be able
to make good choices and decisions
even when my friends do not,
and to stick with my good choices.

At Confirmation, I will receive the gifts of th

Wisdom
helps me to see things from God's point of view.

Understanding
grows as I pray at Mass and Reconciliation.
It helps me know Jesus and follow his example.

Right judgement
helps me to make good choices —
even when it is hard.

Courage
helps me overcome fear and do what is right.

oly Spirit to help me through my whole life!

Knowledge
to be able take to heart
and live all that I learn about God.

Reverence
to love and worship and respect
the holy things of God.

Fear of the Lord
is a holy fear of offending God, our Father,
whom I love.
It makes me want to be close to God
and avoid sin.

I will continue to live with Jesus
through my whole life.

Jesus loves us all and he promised
he would not leave us, ever.
And I know that what Jesus says is true!

Bye for now!

your book angel
Friel